AF228847

KYLIAN MBAPPÉ

WORLD SOCCER SENSATION

BY TODD KORTEMEIER

Essential Library

An Imprint of Abdo Publishing
abdobooks.com

ABDOBOOKS.COM

Published by Abdo Publishing, a division of ABDO, PO Box 398166, Minneapolis, Minnesota 55439. Copyright © 2020 by Abdo Consulting Group, Inc. International copyrights reserved in all countries. No part of this book may be reproduced in any form without written permission from the publisher. Essential Library™ is a trademark and logo of Abdo Publishing.

Printed in the United States of America, North Mankato, Minnesota.
042019
092019

Cover Photo: Michel Euler/AP Images
Interior Photos: Frank Hoermann/Sven Simon/picture-alliance/dpa/AP Images, 4; Thanassis Stavrakis/AP Images, 8; Lionel Hahn/Abaca/Sipa USA/AP Images, 10; Cezaro De Luca/picture-alliance/dpa/AP Images, 12; Lionel Cironneau/AP Images, 14, 26; Henri Szwarc/Abaca/Sipa USA/AP Images, 18; Laurent Fighiera/Shutterstock Images, 20–21; Shutterstock Images, 22; Szwarc Henri/Sipa USA/AP Images, 29; Deniz Calagan/picture-alliance/dpa/AP Images, 30, 38; Srdjan Stevanovic/Getty Images Sport/Getty Images, 33; Deniz Calagan/picture alliance/Getty Images, 36; Uwe Anspach/picture-alliance/dpa/AP Images, 40; Claude Paris/AP Images, 42; Christophe Saidi/Sipa/AP Images, 46; Martin Wickett/PA Wire URN:30208131/Press Association/AP Images, 48; Bernd Thissen/picture-alliance/dpa/AP Images, 51; David Niviere/Sipa/AP Images, 54; Christophe Ena/AP Images, 57, 61, 62; Christian Liewig/Sipa USA/AP Images, 64; Scott Heppell/AP Images, 67; Patrick Clemente/Abaca/Sipa USA/AP Images, 69; Thomas Schmidtutz/AP Images, 70; Ugo Amez/Sipa/AP Images, 74; J.E.E./Spia USA/AP Images, 77; Pro Shots Photo Agency/Sipa USA/AP Images, 78, 89; Hassan Ammar/AP Images, 81; Alizada Studios/AP Images, 84; Petr David Josek/AP Images, 86; Rafael Yaghobzadeh/Abaca Press/Sipa USA/AP Images, 90; Lodi Franck/Sipa USA/AP Images, 93; Christian Liewig/Abaca Press/Sipa USA/AP Images, 96

Editor: Patrick Donnelly
Series Designer: Laura Graphenteen

LIBRARY OF CONGRESS CONTROL NUMBER: 2018967355

PUBLISHER'S CATALOGING-IN-PUBLICATION DATA

Names: Kortemeier, Todd, author.
Title: Kylian Mbappe: world soccer sensation / by Todd Kortemeier
Other title: World soccer sensation
Description: Minneapolis, Minnesota: Abdo Publishing, 2020 | Series: Star athletes | Includes online resources and index.
Identifiers: ISBN 9781532119903 (lib. bdg.) | ISBN 9781532174735 (ebook) | ISBN 9781644940976 (pbk.)
Subjects: LCSH: Mbappé, Kylian, 1998---Juvenile literature. | Soccer players--France--Biography--Juvenile literature. | Paris-Saint-Germain-Football-Club--Juvenile literature. | Sports--Biography--Juvenile literature.
Classification: DDC 796.334092 [B]--dc23

CONTENTS

COMEBACK KID

In 2018, both the French and Argentinian national teams had won the World Cup before. But because the two world powerhouses were facing off in the first Round of 16 matchup, only one of them would advance to the quarterfinals of the 2018 World Cup.

Each was trying to win the cup after a long layoff. France had won its most recent title on home soil 20 years earlier. For Argentina, it had been 32 years. The team's hopes were tied to forward Lionel Messi, one of the greatest players in the world.

Any conversation about how far Argentina could advance began and ended with Messi. But by the end of the match, nobody would be talking about Messi. They would be talking about the world's *next* superstar, Kylian Mbappe. And he played for France.

Kylian Mbappe came through in style at his first World Cup.

MBAPPE VS. MESSI

Mbappe and Messi were both among the youngest players ever to play for their respective countries. Both were teenagers when they made their World Cup debuts. Each came onto the world stage as a potential superstar in the making. But Mbappe made more of an impact in his first World Cup. Messi played in just three of five Argentina matches in 2006. He scored one goal, making him the sixth-youngest goal scorer in World Cup history at 18 years, 11 months, and 23 days. Mbappe became the twelfth youngest when he scored against Peru. He was 19 years, six months, and one day. The youngest in history was Pelé, who was just over 17 and one-half.

HIGH EXPECTATIONS

Mbappe was only 19. But the soccer world had already known about him for years from his heroics with his club teams, AS Monaco and Paris Saint-Germain (PSG) of France's Ligue 1. He made his Ligue 1 debut at 16, becoming the youngest Monaco player ever. It was one of Mbappe's numerous youth-related milestones, including becoming the second-youngest-ever player for the French national team.

But could he handle the huge stage that was the World Cup? Carrying a team to a world championship was a lot to ask of a teenager. So far, he had played a crucial role for the Blues—or Les Bleus, as they are called, because of their bright blue jerseys. In a group stage match against Peru, he scored the only goal in a 1–0 win.

That game was revealing of France's performance as a whole in the group stage. It needed an own goal by Australia to prevail in its opening match, 2–1. Then after narrowly beating Peru, the French managed a scoreless draw with Denmark. It was enough to allow them to advance, but their group-stage performance raised questions about how far they could advance in the knockout rounds.

"It's a new tournament now, and it's make or break," said France coach Didier Deschamps before facing Argentina.[1]

The desperation of both teams to keep their World Cup dreams alive was clear as soon as the match started. Just under ten minutes in, Mbappe drew a foul in the offensive zone. Teammate Antoine Griezmann took the free kick and rang it off the crossbar. But just a few minutes later, Mbappe won another foul. This time, it

WORLD CUP COACH

The Argentina match was the eightieth for France coach Didier Deschamps. With it, he became the longest-serving coach in the history of the national team. Deschamps knew a thing or two about winning a World Cup. He was a defensive midfielder on the 1998 France team. Deschamps made 103 appearances for France before he retired in 2000. After retiring, he watched France have its worst World Cup performance ever in 2002. France did not score a single goal and finished 28th out of 32 teams. Seeing how that team played so poorly after winning it all helped him when he became coach of France in 2012. He stressed to his players the attitude of never taking anything for granted.

Mbappe, left, is fouled by Argentina's Marcos Rojo, earning a penalty kick for France.

was in the 18-yard box. His effort was rewarded with a penalty kick.

Griezmann again stepped up and took the kick. He blasted it past Argentina's goalkeeper to make the score 1–0 France. But the Argentinians were not deterred.

They hung on and eventually tied the match just before halftime. France had the majority of possession and felt in control. But it was still anybody's game.

TAKING OVER

France would need Mbappe's speed and elusiveness in the second half. Argentina kept him off the score sheet but could not keep him from getting the ball. Seemingly the only way to stop Mbappe was to foul him. If he could just finish his opportunities and convert them into goals, France would be on its way to victory.

But just after halftime, disaster struck. France failed to clear a ball properly in its own half. Messi collected it and fired a shot on goal. It deflected off teammate Gabriel Mercado and into the net to give Argentina the lead. For the first time all tournament, France was behind.

The Blues then went on the attack. Within ten minutes, Benjamin Pavard received a crossing pass from the left and put away the tying goal. The Argentina defense was having

DON'T BLINK

Argentina was helpless all game against Mbappe's speed. He not only could move quickly but also was almost impossible to catch at top speed. On a run that led to France's first goal, Mbappe ran 230 feet (70 m) in seven seconds. His top speed was 24 miles per hour (39 kmh). That was the fastest speed recorded at the tournament. It was only slightly slower than gold-medal sprinter Usain Bolt.[2]

Mbappe and teammate Antoine Griezmann celebrate a goal against Argentina.

trouble keeping up with France's pace. It was time for Mbappe to make his mark.

Seven minutes after the tying goal, France's Lucas Hernandez sent the ball in front of the goal. Blaise Matuidi's shot was blocked. The ball fell to Mbappe. He deftly poked it between two Argentina defenders. Then, with a third player closing in, Mbappe got off a shot with his left foot. It had enough speed to get under the hand of Argentina keeper Franco Armani. Just like that, France led 3–2.

ONE MORE

Mbappe was not done. Four minutes later, France was on the counterattack. Matuidi carried the ball upfield. He passed it to Olivier Giroud. Meanwhile, Mbappe was making a dashing run up the right side. Giroud took one look to his right and poked the ball past an Argentina defender. The ball rolled perfectly in front of Mbappe to where he could get a full strike on it. His shot rocketed past Armani for a 4–2 lead.

France's substitutes, who were warming up on the sideline, ran onto the field to mob Mbappe. He was the first teenager since Brazilian great Pelé in 1958 to score two goals in a World Cup knockout match.

"I'm very happy," Mbappe said after the match. "It's flattering to be second after Pelé. But let's put things in context: Pelé is another category. But it's good to be among these people who score in knockouts."[3]

With a two-goal lead, it looked as if France had done enough to advance. It had to hold the lead for

approximately 20 more minutes. Near the end of the match, Mbappe was replaced by a substitute. France did not need any more goals.

However, Argentina would not go quietly. Three minutes into stoppage time, Sergio Aguero scored to make it 4–3. But France held on for the last few minutes. Mbappe was named Man of the Match, and France was on to the quarterfinals.

Mbappe was born in the year France had last won the World Cup. It was fitting that he was in a position to lead France to another title.

WORLD CUP THRILLER

The France-Argentina match was one of the most exciting of the 2018 World Cup. The teams combined to put eight shots on target, and seven of them went in for goals. Only Messi took a shot that was stopped. Just two other matches at the 2018 World Cup featured seven goals scored. But this was the only one-goal game among them. Soccer fans all over the world were thrilled. Even tennis star Andy Murray lamented that he was missing the match while competing at Wimbledon. Mbappe's performance drew a lot of attention. English great Gary Lineker tweeted that Mbappe was the next world superstar.

Lionel Messi, left, congratulates Mbappe after France knocked out Argentina at the 2018 World Cup.

YOUTH CAREER

Bondy is a town located just a few miles north of Paris. But despite being so close, Bondy looks a lot different from the French capital. It is a small, working-class community. Many of its inhabitants are immigrants and other people of color.

Kylian Adesanmi Mbappe Lottin was born in Paris on December 20, 1998, but he grew up in Bondy. His father, Wilfried, was from Cameroon. His mother, Fayza, was from Algeria. Both of those countries were once colonies of France.

Many people came to France from these countries. They settled near Paris in suburbs called *banlieues*. Some French people looked down on these communities and people like Kylian. Even though he was born in France, they judged him and others like him by the color of their skin.

Kylian Mbappe reacts after scoring a goal for Monaco.

Like so many French kids, those in the banlieues dreamed of being soccer stars. Kylian was no different. Lining his bedroom walls were posters of his hero, the legendary Cristiano Ronaldo of Portugal.

Kylian came from an athletic family. Both his parents were associated with the local AS Bondy sports club. Fayza was a top player for the club's handball team. Wilfried was a soccer player and then became a coach for the club.

Wilfried was still a coach there while Kylian was growing up. The club's senior team was not very good. But its youth programs were excellent. Kylian had spent time around the club since he was a baby.

"I work in [soccer] and [Kylian] almost puts me off it because he's always into it 24/7. He watches everything; he can watch four or five matches in a row."[1]
— Wilfried Mbappe

A CLEAR TALENT

As early as the age of two, Kylian would sit in on team meetings and learn about the game. He started officially playing for a Bondy youth team in 2004 when he was six.

But Kylian played all the time, even beyond his team's games. He would even set up games in the family living room, against the wishes of his parents.

Kylian's smooth moves on the field were clear from a young age. Coaches saw him performing incredible stepover moves when he was seven and eight years old. It was hard for Kylian to find fair competition. He often played against older kids just to find a challenge.

Kylian's talent did not stay a secret for long. When he was 11, he had a trial with Chelsea in London, England. Chelsea was one of the greatest clubs in the world and played in England's Premier League. Chelsea hoped to recruit Kylian. He spent one week at the club, but he didn't want to leave France to join Chelsea. As he got older, more and more clubs had an interest in signing him.

When he was 13, in 2011, Kylian started attending Clairefontaine Academy while continuing to play with Bondy. Clairefontaine is a boarding school that specializes

BIG BROTHER

Kylian is not the only pro soccer player in his family. Before he made a name for himself, he was known as the brother of Jires Kembo-Ekoko. Kembo-Ekoko was adopted by the Mbappe family a few years before Kylian was born. Kembo-Ekoko was born in Zaire, known today as the Democratic Republic of the Congo. His father had played for Zaire at the 1974 World Cup. He was sent to live with an uncle in France, where he later was adopted by Wilfried Mbappe while playing youth soccer in Bondy. Kembo-Ekoko went on to a pro soccer career, playing mostly with Rennes in France.

Kylian's portrait hangs inside Clairefontaine Academy.

in developing soccer players. Numerous French national team players attended the academy as young boys.

Kylian had all the skills of a great player. But he was still young and thin. At Clairefontaine, he grew bigger and stronger while developing his soccer skills even more.

Kylian took soccer seriously. But he also knew when to relax and have fun. He and his teammates played soccer in their dormitories at night. They used a soft ball so they would not get caught. The boys sometimes got in trouble for that. But Kylian just loved to play and have fun.

CLUBS COME CALLING

Once Kylian became bigger and stronger, the interest from other clubs grew as well. Chelsea was still interested. Some other big clubs in England and Germany were after Kylian, too.

But Real Madrid might have wanted him the most. Real was one of the biggest clubs in the world. That was where Ronaldo played. One of Real's coaches was legendary French player Zinedine Zidane. He met personally with Kylian to try to convince him to play in Madrid.

ELITE ACADEMY

Clairefontaine is an exclusive academy for only the best soccer players in France. Founded in 1988, only 23 players are admitted each year. Players from the Paris region ages 13 to 15 are eligible to play. Clairefontaine is also the home training ground of the French national team. The academy has developed some of the most famous names in national team history, including Mbappe, Thierry Henry, Nicolas Anelka, and William Gallas. Some members of the 2018 World Cup team came from Clairefontaine, including Blaise Matuidi.

Kylian chose to play for Monaco, which is located on the Mediterranean Sea. The soccer stadium, lower right, was built in the 1980s.

"He was always out there doing extra practice. He's our mascot. He's proof that, if you work hard enough, everything is possible."[3]
—16-year-old Ayoub, who grew up in Bondy watching Kylian play

It was a tough offer to turn down. But Kylian wasn't ready to leave home quite yet. He signed with the youth academy of Association Sportive (AS) Monaco in 2013.

The AS Monaco academy had developed many great French players. Four players

from the 1998 World Cup team played there. Playing for Monaco allowed Kylian to stay close to home while still playing at a high level.

Kylian starred with Monaco's Under-19 team. At one point, he scored two or more goals six matches in a row. That performance earned him a spot on the Monaco reserve team. Although he was only 16, his career was progressing rapidly.

AS MONACO FC

MONACO
ROOKIE

Among French soccer players, there are few bigger names than Thierry Henry. The striker earned 123 caps for France and won the World Cup with Les Bleus in 1998. His 51 goals are the most in French history. He was a global superstar whose career began in Monaco and took him to some of the biggest clubs in the world in Juventus, Arsenal, and Barcelona.

When Kylian Mbappe made his AS Monaco senior team debut in 2015, he immediately began to draw comparisons to Henry. Both were supreme goal scorers who were educated at Clairefontaine and began their careers with Monaco.

Mbappe started knocking down Henry's records right away. After playing five games for the Monaco reserve team and scoring two goals, Mbappe made his senior team debut on December 2, 2015. He came on as a substitute in

Kylian Mbappe was just 16 years old when he debuted for AS Monaco's senior team.

MONACO

While AS Monaco plays in the French league, it is located in a completely separate country. The country of Monaco is surrounded on all sides by French territory, except for the part that borders the Mediterranean Sea. It is located in the southeastern corner of France, and its eastern border is just a few miles from Italy. Monaco is the second-smallest country in the world after Vatican City. The country is perhaps most famous for hosting the Grand Prix of Monaco Formula One race. That race is one of the most famous auto events in the world.

"What he's showing for his age is interesting. But the path is long. I've seen others before who didn't come through. He has to be attentive and make the right choices."[1]
— former Monaco captain Jeremy Toulalan

the eighty-eighth minute of a 1–1 draw with Caen. At 16 years and 347 days old, he broke Henry's record for the youngest player in Monaco history.

Mbappe was on the bench for Monaco's next league match and came on as a sub again in two matches after that. He got his first chance to start for Monaco on December 16. He played the entirety of Monaco's Coupe de la Ligue match with Bordeaux. The Coupe de la Ligue is a season-long tournament just for French teams. Monaco beat Bordeaux 3–0.

THE FIRST GOAL

While Mbappe was getting playing time, he had yet to find his way onto the score sheet. That changed in the dying moments of a league match against Troyes on February 20, 2016. Mbappe had come on in the seventy-third minute. Monaco was holding a 2–1 lead in the ninety-third minute. As Troyes was working the ball up the field trying to tie the match, the team turned it over.

As soon as that happened, Mbappe broke from his position in midfield and streaked toward the goal. Nobody was guarding him. He was wide open at the top of the 18-yard box. His Monaco teammate spotted him and rolled a pass right into his path. Mbappe hammered the ball with his left foot and beat the keeper.

Mbappe raised his arms in celebration, and his teammates quickly surrounded him. He was still such a new player that he did not even have his name on the back of his jersey. Mbappe had just turned 17 in December.

At 17 years, 62 days, he was the youngest player to score a goal in Monaco history. Again, it was Henry's record that he broke. Henry was 17 years, 254 days old when he scored against Lens in April 1995.

STADE LOUIS II

Monaco's home stadium is the Stade Louis II. The first Stade Louis II opened in 1939, and the current one was constructed nearby in 1985. The stadium is named for Louis II, Prince of Monaco. It seats approximately 18,500 fans, which is about half the entire population of Monaco. The stadium is very close to the Mediterranean Sea. A street runs just behind the west end of the stadium that forms the border between Monaco and France.

AFFL
FED
33
LFP
NIKE
TRIANGLE

STAYING IN MONACO

The goal against Troyes was the only one Mbappe scored that season. But his play was impressive enough that Monaco offered him a contract just a few days later. The club did so knowing that some bigger clubs were still hoping to sign the young academy player and steal him out from under Monaco's nose.

But Mbappe again rejected the other clubs. He signed his first professional contract with Monaco on March 6, 2016. He believed that Monaco was still the best place for him to develop into a world-class player.

AS MONACO HISTORY

AS Monaco was formed from a merger of five teams in 1919. But it took a while for the club to become competitive. It did not win promotion to the First Division (now known as Ligue 1) until 1953. The club won its first league title in 1961. Legendary coach Arsene Wenger got his start at the club, leading Monaco to a championship in his first season in 1987–88. The club has had numerous great players in its history, such as George Weah, Jürgen Klinsmann, Thierry Henry, and Patrice Evra.

"There isn't a better project in Europe for young players than Monaco."[2]
— Club vice president Vadim Vasilyev, in advocating for Mbappe to remain with the club.

Mbappe (33) is swarmed by his teammates after he scored his first goal for Monaco on February 20, 2016.

TRANSFERS

Players change teams in European soccer a little differently than in major North American sports. Instead of being traded or signing with new teams as free agents, players are usually transferred. That means one club pays another club for the rights to sign one of its players. The club then negotiates a contract with the player, including what he is going to be paid. Transfers are allowed in only two periods—or transfer windows—each year. One lasts from July 1 to August 31, and the other consists of the entire month of January.

"This is the club that has helped me grow," Mbappe said. "I feel good here, and I'm going to be able to continue taking new steps forward."[3]

Mbappe finished the season with one goal in 14 appearances. The club finished third in Ligue 1. But with Mbappe on board, things were looking up. Monaco fans could not wait to see what he would do in his first full season with the club.

Mbappe, left, battles with David Luiz of Paris Saint-Germain during a Ligue 1 match in March 2016.

WEARING THE BLUE

Kylian Mbappe had dreamed of playing for the French national team for much of his life. Though he was not born when France last won the World Cup, he grew up watching legends such as Thierry Henry and Zinedine Zidane. As soon as he became known as one of the top talents in France, he was on the fast track to the national team.

Mbappe's first brush with Les Bleus came in 2014 when he was chosen to play for the France Under-17 (U-17) team. But Mbappe did not get many opportunities. The coach of the U-17 squad favored other players over Mbappe and did not choose him to compete at the Under-17 European Championships.

Mbappe also got passed over for the U-18 team. But in 2016, he was selected to the U-19 team that would compete at the U-19 European Championships that summer. Though he was on

Kylian Mbappe was one of the star players for France at the U-19 European Championships in 2016.

Mbappe took an unusual and fast path to the French national team. Despite not playing for France's U-17 and U-18 teams, he went from the U-19 team to the senior team playing at the World Cup in less than two years. Mbappe was the only player selected from the 2016 U-19 side to play in the 2018 FIFA World Cup. He was in the mix to be chosen for the U-20 team in 2017 that would play at the U-20 World Cup. But senior team head coach Didier Deschamps wanted to keep him so that Mbappe could focus on World Cup qualifying.

the U-19 team, Mbappe was still just 17. He was two years younger than many of his teammates. He may not have been the biggest and strongest player, but coaches saw that his advanced skills fit in on the team.

"He has an ability to express and analyze that I have rarely seen in kids of this age," said U-19 head coach Ludovic Batelli.[1]

ENSURING A PLACE

Before the U-19 European Championships kicked off in the summer, France had to qualify. In the middle of his debut season for Monaco, Mbappe traveled with the U-19s to Serbia. They had to finish first in their group in order to move on and play for the championship.

France won a close 1–0 game over Montenegro in its first game. Then, in the second game, Mbappe opened the scoring as France routed Denmark 4–0. With a 2–0 record, France was in good shape to move on. But

Mbappe takes a shot on goal against Serbia during a U-19 European Championships qualifying match.

Mbappe made sure of that by scoring the only goal in a 1–0 win over Serbia in the team's last game.

After Monaco's season concluded, Mbappe rejoined the U-19s to get ready for the European Championships. The tournament was held in Germany. France had been one of the most successful teams in the tournament's history. Going into the 2016 edition, the Blues had seven titles, the third most of any nation.

FRENCH SOCCER

With approximately two million players, soccer is the most popular sport in France. It is also extremely popular among fans, as Ligue 1 is on average the eighth-best-attended league in the world. In the 2017–18 season, an average of 21,199 fans attended each Ligue 1 match.[2] Soccer in France dates back to 1872, with the first organized competition beginning in 1894. France hosted the World Cup in 1938 and 1998 and the Women's World Cup in 2019.

Youth tournaments are very important for countries. The nations with the best young players often see that pay off down the road. Those young players often make a difference on the senior teams and hopefully at the World Cup.

France had not won the World Cup since 1998. The French were looking to rebuild their national team, and they were counting on players like Mbappe to play important roles. He started every game in Germany.

MBAPPE AND AUGUSTIN

France lost a heartbreaking opener 2–1 to rival England. Mbappe was substituted in the sixtieth minute and did not score a goal. It was one of the few games in which he did not make an impact.

Needing a win to get back on track, France faced Croatia. As good as Mbappe was, France did not have to rely on him alone. He had a forward partner in Jean-Kevin

Augustin, who had scored the lone goal in the loss
to England.

The duo combined to lead France against Croatia.
Augustin opened the scoring in the thirty-seventh minute.
France held the 1–0 lead into halftime.

Croatia had also lost its first game. Both teams were
desperate to get points. But neither squad could break
through to score. Then Mbappe showed the world what
he could do. He used all the skills he was famous for to get
France the goal it needed.

In the sixty-ninth minute, France had a free kick from
midfield. As soon as the ball was kicked toward the goal,
Mbappe took off. He used his blazing speed to reach the
ball and establish inside position on the defender. Another
defender came over to help, but Mbappe dribbled
through them both.

That left him alone on the goalkeeper. Mbappe
used his tremendous control to tap the ball to his left.
The keeper went to the ground and could not catch up.
Mbappe dribbled around him and fired the ball into the
open net. France held on for a 2–0 victory.

Mbappe fights off a hard challenge from a Croatia defender at the U-19 European Championships.

ADVANCING

The win gave France three points, tied with the Netherlands. The Netherlands happened to be France's opponent in its final group-stage match. Either a tie or a win would put France into the knockout stage. But a loss could send the team home.

Just as he had in Serbia, Mbappe made sure that did not happen. He opened the scoring in the tenth minute. After a teammate made a darting run toward goal, Mbappe found himself alone at the top of the 6-yard box. He took the pass and fired the ball home with his right foot.

Augustin doubled the lead in the twenty-ninth minute. But seven minutes later, the Dutch were awarded a penalty and converted. France held a narrow 2–1 lead at half.

But from there, the Blues pulled away. Augustin doubled the lead just after halftime. A teammate was trying to pick out Mbappe in the 18-yard box, but the ball fell into Augustin's path instead. He did not miss.

Then, in the sixty-third minute, the dynamic duo was at it again. Augustin was running on goal but fired a pass across the box to Mbappe, who put it away with his right foot. The keeper drove to his right but caught nothing but air. Augustin scored again in the seventy-fifth minute to complete his hat trick and a 5–1 rout of the Netherlands.

Mbappe makes a move against Netherlands goalkeeper Yannick van Osch during France's big victory.

MAKING THE FINAL

It was an emphatic statement by France. The team intended to win the whole tournament. Its opponent in the semifinals was Portugal. But instead of taking the early lead, France was stunned when Portugal scored in the opening five minutes.

Les Bleus quickly gathered themselves, however. In the tenth minute, Mbappe was streaking down the goal line when he found Ludovic Blas in front of the goal to tie the match. The score remained tied until late in the match. Then Mbappe took over again to see France through.

Through his parents, Mbappe is eligible to represent either Cameroon or Algeria. Because he was born in France, he also could play for the Blues. Kylian's father wanted him to play for Cameroon. But the Cameroon soccer federation wanted to charge Kylian's family money to allow him to play for them. France did not charge them anything. Kylian went on to proudly represent the country of his birth.

In the sixty-seventh minute, Mbappe received a long crossing pass and found himself one-on-one against the goalkeeper. He used a delicate touch with his right foot to just tip it past the keeper.

Mbappe was not done. But the next time, he used his head. Just about eight minutes later, France had a throw-in in its own end. The powerful throw came all the way into the 6-yard box, where Mbappe was jumping with a teammate.

Mbappe outjumped his defender, sending a header past the keeper and giving France a 3–1 late lead. Mbappe ran down the sideline screaming in celebration and pumping his fist. At the final whistle, he and his

teammates celebrated again as they booked a place in July's championship game.

Mbappe's five goals tied him with Augustin for the most in the tournament. In the final against Italy, Augustin scored one more to secure the tournament lead. Mbappe did not score as France won 4–0, but he was a huge part of getting the team there.

While his teammates went out to party after the game, Mbappe decided to stay home and go to bed. He was thrilled to be a European champion. But he was already thinking about all the other goals he wanted to achieve.

FUTURE SUCCESS

Many French players have gone on to success with the senior national team after winning the U-19 Euro title, including three star players on France's 2018 World Cup team. Goalkeeper Hugo Lloris won the title in 2005, while Antoine Griezmann and Alexandre Lacazette (an alternate for the World Cup team) were teammates in 2010. By winning the European Championship, France qualified to compete at the 2017 U-20 World Cup. Most of the team from the 2016 Euros played at the World Cup as well—minus Mbappe—but lost in the Round of 16 to Italy. France has been less successful in that competition historically, winning its only title in 2013.

Mbappe celebrates his goal against Portugal in the semifinals.

MON
2017 CHAMPIONS
UNIQUE
FOREVER
NOTRE FOI EST...
QUE NUL NE PEUT...
DEPUIS 1994
GUE 1

CHAMPION OF
FRANCE

Since the early 1960s, AS Monaco had been one of the top clubs in Ligue 1, winning seven league titles entering the 2016–17 season. But its most recent championship came in 2000. The club even had been moved to a lower league in 2011 because of financial problems.

But things were looking up by 2016. The club was coming off back-to-back third-place finishes in the league. And it had Kylian Mbappe.

While the club had historic success in Ligue 1, it had not been as successful in the Union of European Football Associations (UEFA) Champions League. The Champions League is a yearlong tournament for the top clubs in Europe. Entry is determined by the domestic league standings of the various countries in the previous season. Monaco had never won the Champions League, only finishing second once. But the club would

Monaco players celebrate their 2017 Ligue 1 title.

chase titles in both Ligue 1 and the Champions League in 2016–17.

Monaco was able to rely on Mbappe as a major part of the team. Unlike in the previous year, in which he played in only 14 matches, Mbappe was a regular player in 2016–17. He started the first league match of the year in August, though he suffered an injury that kept him out of the starting lineup again until October.

He returned with a goal in a 6–2 win over Montpellier in Ligue 1. But whether it was due to injury or playing in one of the world's best leagues at 17 years old, Mbappe struggled to find his scoring touch.

MAKING PROGRESS

When a goal scorer advances to a new level of competition, it often takes time to start scoring a lot. Mbappe was no different. In his first season with Monaco in 2015–16, Mbappe had two assists and just a single goal. The next year, with a lot more playing time, Mbappe scored 26 goals. He also contributed 11 assists. By the time he turned 20, Mbappe had played a role in 62 Ligue 1 goals, scoring 41 and assisting on 21 others. That was 36 more than any other player his age or younger playing in any of Europe's top five leagues.

GOALS IN BUNCHES

A December Coupe da la Ligue match against Rennes helped get him going. Mbappe became the first Monaco player in almost 20 years to score a hat trick in that competition as Monaco won 7–0.

Mbappe did it again in a Ligue 1 match in February. At 18 years and two months, he was the youngest player to score a hat trick in Ligue 1 since 2005. The 5–0 win over Metz was big for Mbappe but even bigger for Monaco. They went three points ahead in first place of Ligue 1, putting them in good shape to win the title.

But Mbappe was just getting started. In his next eight matches, he scored nine goals. And they were huge ones as Monaco looked to win trophies. On March 1, he scored in a 4–3 win over Marseille that advanced Monaco in the Coupe de France. He scored three goals in back-to-back league wins over Nantes and Bordeaux.

MAGIC vs. MAN CITY

Then came a huge Champions League showdown against English power Manchester City. It was the second of two matches between the two in the Round of 16. The club that scored the most combined goals in both

Mbappe fights off a defender from Chambly in a Coupe de France match in February 2017.

matches—or legs, as they are known—would advance to the quarterfinals. The first leg was played in England in February, and the second would take place in Monaco in March. Mbappe scored in the first match in Manchester.

That goal would prove to be important, even though Manchester City won 5–3.

In the second leg, Monaco knew that it had to score a lot to overcome the deficit. Mbappe did not waste any time. In the eighth minute, a Manchester City defender blocked a shot. It deflected back to a Monaco player, who fired it back toward goal where Mbappe was waiting. He kicked his right foot out and deflected it into the goal. It was a great start, but Monaco needed more goals.

Monaco doubled its lead in the twenty-ninth minute. That made the aggregate score 5–5, but because Monaco had scored three goals in England, it actually was winning. That's because in the event of a tie, the club that scored the most goals as a visitor would be used to break the tie. As long as Monaco could keep the total score tied, it would advance in the Champions League.

Manchester City scored late in the second half to take a 6–5 lead in aggregate, but Monaco responded

almost immediately to tie it up again. The English club was unable to get another goal, and Monaco moved on. Mbappe's team was among the final eight standing in the tournament.

Back in Ligue 1, Mbappe scored his ninth and tenth goals of the season in his next match. He was the youngest player in three decades to score at least ten league goals.

MAKING THE QUARTERS

Champions League play resumed in April with Monaco facing Borussia Dortmund of Germany. It was another two-leg contest. The first leg was in Dortmund. In the seventeenth minute, Mbappe was streaking toward goal, but he was brought down by a Dortmund defender. The referee awarded a penalty kick for the foul. Monaco's Fabinho took the kick but missed it wide.

Mbappe erased that disappointment two minutes later. He made an excellent run into the box to get open but failed to get a good strike on the ball. Instead, it hit off his thigh, but that was enough to beat the keeper and give Monaco a 1–0 lead.

Mbappe scores a critical goal at Manchester during Monaco's Champions League clash with Manchester City.

OLD AND NEW

Against Juventus in the 2016–17 Champions League semifinal, Mbappe was trying his best to score on keeper Gianluigi Buffon. The Italian legend was 39 years old. He was playing in the World Cup final months before Mbappe was even born. Though they shared the same field in the Champions League, they were of two different generations. They actually became teammates in 2018 playing for Paris Saint-Germain (PSG).

After a Dortmund own goal, Monaco led 2–0 at halftime. Dortmund got on the board in the fifty-seventh minute before Mbappe used his trademark speed to get Monaco back on top. As a Dortmund player tried to move the ball upfield, Mbappe quickly took the ball away from him. He then sped away and took a shot one-on-one against the goalkeeper. He fired it into the top-right corner for a 3–1 lead. Monaco held on for a 3–2 win. It was in that game that Mbappe unveiled his famous goal celebration. He crossed his arms in front of him as he slid toward the corner of the field on his knees. Mbappe had learned the celebration from his younger brother, Ethan, who used it against Mbappe after beating him in a soccer video game.

In the second leg, Mbappe was there for Monaco again. And again, he was there quickly. In the third minute, a Monaco teammate fired a shot on goal. The keeper

Mbappe breaks out his new goal celebration after scoring against Borussia Dortmund in Champions League play.

einsbank
B.DE/EX SIVKONTO
RESPECT

saved it, but Mbappe was right there. He hammered in the rebound for a 1–0 lead in the match and 4–2 lead in total. Monaco went on to win the match 3–1 and advanced with a 6–3 aggregate victory.

BITTERSWEET END

Mbappe scored a goal in the second leg of the semifinals against Juventus, but it was not enough. Monaco lost 4–1 on aggregate score and was eliminated from the Champions League. Still, making the semifinal was the club's best performance in the competition since making the final in 2004. And Mbappe scored six goals in his first nine matches. That was the best performance for a Monaco player since Henry.

Monaco did not finish the season empty-handed, however. Thanks in part to Mbappe's 15 league goals, Monaco won Ligue 1 for the eighth time in team history. He scored his fifteenth in the second-to-last game of the year to clinch the title. In all, Mbappe scored 26 goals in 44 matches.

Once again, the biggest clubs in the world came calling, hoping to pry Mbappe away from Monaco. He was under contract, but Monaco could opt to sell him to another team. The club knew, however, that players like Mbappe were rare.

"Mbappe has no price," said Monaco's club vice president, Vadim Vasilyev. "He is like a son."[2]

It was up to Mbappe to decide where he wanted to take the next step in his career.

LES BLEUS DEBUT

As if Kylian Mbappe wasn't busy enough helping Monaco win Ligue 1, he also got his first chance to play for the French national team in March 2017. Just one day after scoring to help knock Manchester City out of the Champions League, Mbappe debuted with France in a World Cup qualifying match.

France was undefeated in World Cup qualifying to that point. And tiny Luxembourg was not expected to challenge them at all. It was a good time for Mbappe to get some experience in a meaningful match.

It was not much experience, as Mbappe spent most of the game on the bench. He came on as a substitute in the seventy-eighth minute, just after Olivier Giroud scored his second goal of the day to give France a 3–1 lead.

Kylian Mbappe made his national team debut in 2017.

FRANCE'S AFRICAN PLAYERS

Mbappe was one of several players on France's national team who had African heritage. Most were born in France and had at least one African parent, like Mbappe. But some players, such as goalkeeper Steve Mandanda, were born in Africa but later moved to France. Almost the entire roster had some kind of foreign heritage, even if it was not African. Because of France's colonial history, this was not new. Many French legends, such as Zinedine Zidane and Samir Nasri, had African ancestry.

Mbappe did have one golden chance. Shortly after entering the game, he forced the Luxembourg keeper to make a diving save. France went on to win 3–1. Mbappe had become the second-youngest player ever to play for France at 18 years and 95 days old.

COMING HOME

Three days later, France had a friendly scheduled with Spain. This time, it was going to be at the national team's home, the Stade de France. Located in the Paris suburb of Saint-Denis, the Stade de France was less than a half-hour drive from Mbappe's hometown of Bondy. To make it even more special, Mbappe was starting.

Playing alongside French star Antoine Griezmann,

Olivier Giroud, left, subs in for Mbappe during the friendly against Spain at the Stade de France in Paris.

Mbappe impressed the home fans with his speed and skills. He played 65 minutes before being substituted by Giroud. France lost the match 2–0. But fans were starting to see the potential of what the national team could do.

Mbappe then finished out AS Monaco's 2016–17 title-winning season. The Ligue 1 schedule wrapped up on

EARLY HISTORY

The French national team was founded in 1904. The team played its first game that year, a 3–3 draw with Belgium. The first home match took place the next year, a 1–0 win over Switzerland in front of a reported 500 fans. The national team did not enjoy much success in the early years but qualified for the first World Cup in 1930. Lucien Laurent scored France's first goal in World Cup history with a nineteenth-minute strike against Mexico.

May 20. By early June, Mbappe was training with the national team. An injury kept him out of a friendly with Paraguay, but he came on as a substitute in a World Cup qualifier against Sweden.

Mbappe did not have much of a chance to make an impact, coming on in the seventy-sixth minute. He could not rescue France from a surprising 2–1 loss. France was still in a good position to qualify for the World Cup, but fans were nervous.

A French newspaper ran a poll asking fans who they thought should be on France's World Cup roster. Even though he had barely played for the national team, 97 percent of voters chose Mbappe.[2] They believed he was the future and should play.

Mbappe started and played the entirety of a June 13 friendly against England. He assisted on the game-winning goal by Ousmane Dembele in the seventy-eighth minute. It was an exciting result in front of the home fans.

But that match was just a friendly. The team had to get back on track for World Cup qualifying. Its next match was at the Stade de France against the Netherlands in August.

SCORING ONE FOR FRANCE

France came out firing. Griezmann scored in the fourteenth minute. But it stayed a close match until late. A few minutes after France doubled its lead, Mbappe came on for Giroud.

Mbappe worked hard to get his first international goal. But none of his efforts paid off. France added a third goal in the eighty-eighth minute. Then Mbappe finally got his chance.

He found himself alone against the last Netherlands defender. He got the ball and used all his dribbling tricks to keep the defender off balance and away from him. Mbappe passed to a teammate who passed the ball right back to Mbappe. He struck it with his right foot and buried it.

Mbappe celebrated in front of a full stadium of flag-waving

GOLDEN BOY

In October 2017, Mbappe was honored with the Golden Boy award. The award goes to the best player in Europe under 21 years old. It was a big honor. Previous winners of the award include England's Wayne Rooney and Raheem Sterling, as well as France's Paul Pogba and Anthony Martial, both Mbappe's teammates. Mbappe won easily with 291 votes, beating out Ousmane Dembele, who had 149. The award is voted on by sports journalists.

NEW CLEATS

Mbappe signed a contract with Nike to endorse its products. In 2017, he received his first line of custom soccer cleats. The Hypervenom 3 came in Monaco colors and celebrated the club winning its first title in 17 years. Fans were able to buy the shoes, too. Nike will continue to release special-edition cleats for Mbappe throughout the length of his contract.

"We have to go to Russia. It's more than a goal, it's a fact."[3]
— Kylian Mbappe discussing the urgency he felt as France tried to qualify for the World Cup, which would take place in Russia

fans. He finally had his first international goal. Mbappe started in a scoreless draw with Luxembourg a few days later, and France was on the brink of qualifying for the World Cup. It officially qualified in October after beating Belarus 2–1.

The World Cup was less than a year away. Coach Didier Deschamps had some hard decisions to make about which players would be on that roster. Mbappe clearly showed he had talent. But had he done enough to represent his country at a World Cup? It would be up to Mbappe to show he belonged.

Mbappe controls the ball during France's World Cup qualifier against the Netherlands.

PARIS
MBAPPÉ
29
ooredoo
QNB

BACK IN PARIS

On July 29, 2017, Monaco played Ligue 1 giants Paris Saint-Germain (PSG) in the Trophee des Champions. The annual game matched up the Ligue 1 champions against the winners of the Coupe de France. Kylian Mbappe started the game for Monaco and played 71 minutes of a 2–1 loss.

At the time, Mbappe was again the subject of transfer rumors. It seemed as if Real Madrid was finally going to get its man. It had offered Monaco 180 million euros ($205 million) for the right to sign Mbappe to a contract.[1]

But PSG was a big club, too. Just a few days after the Monaco match, it signed Brazil's Neymar to a five-year contract. Neymar was one of the best players in the world. PSG thought he could help them win the Champions League.

Kylian Mbappe poses with his new Paris Saint-Germain jersey after his transfer from Monaco was official.

Neymar and Mbappe take the field together before their first Ligue 1 match for PSG.

THE PARISIAN

Mbappe chose to go back home rather than join Madrid, the club of his hero, Cristiano Ronaldo. He turned down Madrid "because PSG is the team of my city."[2] Mbappe cost PSG the same 180 million euros offered by Madrid.[3]

"It is with great joy and pride that I join Paris Saint-Germain," Mbappe said. "For any young person from the Paris region, it is often a dream to wear the red and blue jersey and experience the unique atmosphere of the Parc des Princes."[4]

The Parc des Princes, PSG's home stadium, is where fans first got to meet their new hero. Mbappe signed with PSG on August 31. A week later, he was holding up his new PSG jersey in front of fans and under fireworks.

PSG is the only Ligue 1 club in the French capital. Mbappe remembered going to its matches as a boy. The stadium was less than 20 miles (32 km) from Bondy. It really was like coming home.

But expectations were high. PSG paid a lot of money to bring Mbappe to Paris. It was counting on him to score goals and help win matches. Fans expected the same.

Mbappe did not have much time to get adjusted. He was due to play in his first match on September 8 against Metz. He started the match, playing alongside Neymar.

PSG HISTORY

Unlike Monaco, PSG does not trace its history back very far. PSG was founded in 1970 and did not win its first Ligue 1 title until 1986. PSG did not develop into a major club until the 1990s. But since 2010, PSG has emerged as one of the best teams in France, winning six Ligue 1 titles between 2013 and 2019. The club has won eight Ligue 1 titles, 12 Coupe de France titles, and eight Coupe de la Ligue titles.

The new dynamic duo showed what they could do together.

MBAPPE AND NEYMAR

First it was Mbappe. He broke a 1–1 tie in the fifty-ninth minute. The play began with Mbappe trying to chip the ball ahead for Neymar. But the ball got deflected back right into Mbappe's path. He took an easy shot on goal that got past the keeper. Neymar matched his teammate's feat ten minutes later. PSG dominated Metz 5–1.

Mbappe was so hard to stop that a Metz player got a red card after trying to foul him. Ligue 1 opponents already knew about him from his time with Monaco. But now that he was playing with another world-class player in Neymar and a scoring machine in Edinson Cavani, he was even more of a threat. PSG stood atop the Ligue 1 standings after Mbappe's first match with the club.

Mbappe had plenty of reasons to celebrate after his transfer to PSG.

In his next match, Mbappe scored again. It was a 5–0 win over Scottish club Celtic in the Champions League. PSG was a regular participant in the Champions League. But it had never advanced past the quarterfinals. With its new team of stars, it hoped to change that.

"When you buy Neymar, when you buy Mbappe, those are players who make a difference," said teammate Marco Verratti. "It's a signal to us to keep working and to give the maximum."[5]

STRUGGLES

PSG was hard to stop throughout the 2017–18 season. It was clearly the best team in France all year. Only Monaco stayed close. The two powerhouses met in a November league match. For Mbappe, it meant returning to his old home at the Stade Louis II.

It was a return to forget. PSG won 2–1, and the result put them nine points ahead of Monaco. But it was only that close a match because of Mbappe. Ten minutes from the end of the match, Mbappe deflected a Monaco shot into the PSG goal. He also missed a few clear scoring chances.

At one point, he found himself running alone on goal as the ball was passed to him. He had only the keeper to

Mbappe fights for the ball during his return to Monaco with PSG.

beat. But he fired the ball wide left of the goal. Even his former Monaco fans booed the miss.

Mbappe was not scoring, and he wasn't setting teammates up to score either. In his last season in Monaco,

Mbappe scores on a header against Bayern Munich in a Champions League match in 2017.

he had been among the top ten in Ligue 1 for assists. But with PSG, he was often missing teammates or choosing to take more shots himself.

Mbappe got a bit of a break in the next match. He started the game on the bench and came on as a sub in the sixty-ninth minute. But starting with his next game, Mbappe went on another one of his scoring runs. He scored seven goals in his next seven matches.

BACK AGAINST BAYERN

On December 5, he scored in the second leg of a Champions League match against Bayern Munich. His header found the back of the net, cutting the Bayern lead to 2–1. It also made Mbappe the youngest player ever to score ten goals in the Champions League. And it wasn't even close. Mbappe was 18 years, 11 months, and 15 days old. The next youngest player was Lyon's Karim Benzema, who was nearly 21 years old when he scored his tenth Champions League goal in 2008.

PSG lost the Bayern match but still advanced in the Champions League. Most of Mbappe's goals during his seven-game streak came in Ligue 1. But he had his first two-goal game for PSG in the Coupe de France against Rennes.

It was the first match for PSG in more than two weeks. But Mbappe showed no signs of rust. In the ninth minute, he gathered a long pass from midfield in the box. Mbappe let the ball bounce until it was perfectly lined up on his left foot. He then fired it under the goalkeeper for a 1–0 lead.

Then, when it was 3–0 PSG, Mbappe showed his unselfish side. With a golden chance at a goal, he instead played the ball right back to Neymar, who buried it. Mbappe's second goal was an easy one. Defenders paid attention to Angel di Maria, who found Mbappe all alone. All he had to do was tap it into an open goal.

A COSTLY MISTAKE

But things were different the next time PSG played Rennes. This time it was in the Coupe de la Ligue on January 30. With PSG leading 3–0, Mbappe attempted a tackle on Rennes's Ismaila Sarr. Mbappe ended up catching Sarr's calf with the cleats of his shoe. The cleats tore through Sarr's sock as he crumpled to the ground.

The referee showed Mbappe a red card, ejecting him from the match. It was the first red card of his professional career. The 19-year-old treated it as a learning experience.

"There is no need to talk about the referees, they do their job and ours is to play," he said. "I did not do my job today and I was dismissed. That is all."[7]

Mbappe was later suspended for two games. It brought his season to a sudden halt while he was just finding his scoring form. Mbappe had scored 15 goals for PSG so far.

The red card was a rare moment of frustration for Mbappe. His life had changed quite a bit. Still a teenager, he was making more than a million dollars a month. He was so famous that he could not walk down the street in Paris.

But despite all that, Mbappe was a very mature player for his age. He did not score every match, but he often did something else to help his team. Neymar said, "I have the impression that he's already 30, that's how mature and complete he is."[8]

WINNING TROPHIES

Mbappe put his difficulties behind him with another scoring run. PSG was eliminated from the Champions

League on March 6 but was still alive in Ligue 1 and in all of France's cup competitions.

Mbappe helped boost PSG's Ligue 1 position with three goals in two matches. On March 10, Mbappe scored the third goal in a 5–0 rout of Metz. Just before halftime, he used his speed to get behind the defense and receive a pass, easily tucking home the goal.

In the next match against Angers, Mbappe opened the scoring in the twelfth minute with a similar goal to the one against Metz. He waited for the ball, beat his defender to it, and scored. Then he doubled the lead 13 minutes later with a tap-in off a great pass. PSG won 2–1.

On March 31, PSG faced Mbappe's old club for the Coupe de la Ligue title. Mbappe did not score but was a constant threat to Monaco. He was named Man of the Match. He had two assists and also won a penalty kick. Cavani converted it for the first goal of the game. PSG won 3–0. It was the club's second trophy of the season after the Trophee des Champions.

PSG embarrassed Mbappe's former club even more on April 15. Mbappe did not play due to illness, but PSG pounded Monaco 7–1. That win clinched the Ligue 1 title,

Mbappe and Edinson Cavani celebrate PSG's victory over Monaco in the Coupe de la Ligue championship match.

ETHAN MBAPPE

Kylian Mbappe is not the only talented soccer player in his family, and he won't be the last. His brother Ethan, younger by seven years, is a rising star himself. Ethan plays in PSG's youth program. He also is a huge fan of his older brother. He was there with Kylian when he was presented to the PSG fans ahead of the 2017–18 season. He also often attends matches with their father, Wilfried. Kylian and Ethan are often shown hanging out on Kylian's Instagram account.

and it added another trophy to PSG's case. It was the seventh league title in club history.

In the semifinal of the Coupe de France three days later, Mbappe was healthy. He had another two goals in a 3–1 win over Caen. He scored the first goal in the twenty-fifth minute, then put the match away with a goal in the eighty-first.

In the final against Les Herbiers, Mbappe had one shot hit the crossbar and another one blocked. But his teammates finished the job with a 2–0 win. It was the fourth trophy of the season for PSG.

Mbappe finished the season with 21 goals in 44 matches. He added 13 assists. With no possibility of a trade, he was settled in his home. He knew he would be at PSG the next year. But first, he had to worry about winning a world championship.

Mbappe arrives at Clairefontaine in May 2018 to meet his teammates and prepare for the World Cup.

BEST YOUNG PLAYER

There was no more memorable year for French soccer than 1998. The nation hosted that year's World Cup, and the home team won it all. It did this with legendary players such as captain Didier Deschamps and striker Zinedine Zidane.

The team represented a cross section of French society. Some players traced their French ancestry back multiple generations. But many others had ancestors from former French colonies such as Algeria. The team was nicknamed "Black, Blanc, Beur"—French for "black, white, Arab."[1] No matter where people were from, they were all French and could take pride in the team.

Twenty years later, the French national team looked much the same way. Everyone knew about Mbappe. But nine of the 14 players who appeared in the first match of the 2018 World Cup were born

Kylian Mbappe holds the trophy he was awarded as the Best Young Player at the 2018 World Cup.

in either Africa or the Caribbean or had parents who were. Paul Pogba's parents were from Guinea. Samuel Umtiti was born in Cameroon. Blaise Matuidi's father was from Angola, while his mother was Congolese.

France had difficulty in its past integrating people of different races. Also, France doesn't punish discrimination in areas such as housing and jobs as often as the United States and Britain do. In 2005, Mbappe's hometown of Bondy was the site of riots and violence that were related to racial discrimination.

MAKING THE TEAM

Mbappe was officially added to the World Cup squad in May. Deschamps's roster surprised some people. He opted for talented but relatively inexperienced players such as Mbappe and Benjamin Pavard. Longtime international veterans such as Moussa Sissoko and Alexandre Lacazette only made the team as alternates.

HELPING AFRICA

Along with a few other soccer stars of African descent, Mbappe met with French president Emmanuel Macron in 2018. The goal was to initiate a program to support sports in Africa. "Even if I am French, I have African origins," Mbappe said. "Helping African sport develop is important to me. If I can help through my notoriety or others, I will do it with pleasure."[2]

Also in attendance was George Weah. A former soccer player, he went on to become the president of his native Liberia. Weah's son Timothy and Mbappe were teammates on PSG in 2018. Mbappe committed to donating his time and energy to projects that will build sports facilities and operate programs for youth sports in Africa.

In his World Cup debut, Mbappe can't quite get past Australian keeper Patrick Ryan.

There was no doubt France was talented. But could it use that talent to win a world title? France qualified relatively easily but still suffered some losses along the way. The team scheduled three friendlies to get tuned up before the World Cup. Mbappe played in all of them. France beat Ireland 2–0 and Italy 3–1. In the final match against the United States, Mbappe rescued a draw with a late goal.

Down 1–0 in the seventy-eighth minute, Mbappe somehow got the ball in the middle of four US defenders.

The keeper was caught out of position, and Mbappe easily scored. The outcome of the match did not really matter. But Mbappe showed he was ready to come through in key moments.

Just one week later, the World Cup began. It was held in Russia. Still a teenager, Mbappe started France's first match against Australia. At 19 years, 178 days, he was the youngest player ever to play for France at a World Cup.

But he did not have much of an impact on the match. France struggled in the first half. It eventually took the lead in the fifty-eighth minute, but Australia answered four minutes later. It took an Australian own goal to finally give France the lead for good in the eightieth minute.

DOING IT ALONE

It wasn't pretty, but France got the job done. The next match against Peru was similar. France did not create many good scoring chances. Peru actually had possession of the ball longer than France did. But

NATIONAL SYMBOL

The symbol of the French national team is the *coq gaulois* or Gallic rooster. The rooster is also a national symbol of France. In the Middle Ages it was seen as a sign of hope. It became a symbol of France as the nation slowly developed. The French emperor Napoleon tried to change the rooster to an eagle, as he did not think a rooster was a strong enough representative of France. But the country brought it back in the 1800s, and it has been a well-known symbol ever since. When France hosted the World Cup in 1998, its mascot was a rooster named Footix.

Mbappe was there at the right place at the right time to give France a lead.

In the thirty-fourth minute, Pogba took the ball away. He played it forward to Olivier Giroud, who took a shot. The ball bounced off a defender's leg, over the goalkeeper, and right to Mbappe. All he had to do was tap it in. France hung on to win 1–0.

Mbappe had become the youngest player to score a World Cup goal for France. He was named Man of the Match. And with the win, France qualified for the Round of 16.

The final group-stage match did not matter to France too much. But it was another uninspiring performance, a scoreless draw with Denmark. Mbappe came on late as a substitute but was not a factor. Fans in the stadium booed the

HISTORIC YEAR

In 2018, Mbappe scored nine goals for France in 18 matches. That was the most goals for a France player since Thierry Henry scored 11 in 2003. Mbappe also reached ten total international goals. No player had scored that many for Les Bleus at such a young age.

France's starting lineup poses before the World Cup final against Croatia.

boring match. But Deschamps was not worried. He knew what his team could do.

"It was a difficult and challenging group, but we've reached our objective," he said. "Now we have a second phase and we must climb to get to the next level."[4]

They rose to that level through Mbappe. His stunning two-goal performance against Argentina was one of the greatest in French soccer history. Suddenly, France was looking like a World Cup contender.

France had little trouble with Uruguay in the next round. A 2–0 victory booked Les Bleus a place in the semifinals for the first time since 2006. The only blemish was Mbappe being shown a yellow card in the sixty-ninth minute.

Mbappe picked up another yellow in the semifinal match with Belgium. At the World Cup, players who get yellow cards in back-to-back matches have to miss the next match. However, yellow card totals reset after the semifinal. And since France won 1–0, that meant Mbappe did not have to miss the World Cup final.

FINALS BOUND

France's opponent, Croatia, was looking for its first World Cup title. The Croatians had played an exciting tournament. But they also had played a lot of minutes. All three matches since the group stage had gone into extra time. The Croatian players would be fatigued. France was the favorite. But its players had to show they could put a complete game together.

It was another shaky start for France. Croatia controlled the ball more. But then it made a huge mistake. A French shot went in off the head of a Croatian defender in the eighteenth minute. Croatia tied it ten minutes later. But

Mbappe prepares to kick the ball toward the Croatia net in the World Cup final.

then the same player who scored committed a handball, which led to a France penalty kick. Antoine Griezmann buried it, and France took a 2–1 lead into halftime.

France had been in a similar position recently. It was tied with Portugal at halftime of the 2016 European Championship final. It went on to lose the match in extra time. Not all the players had been on that team. But Pogba remembered. He spoke up to encourage his teammates.

"We know we lost a final two years ago," he said. "We know it, we feel it here. It's still in our heads. Today we are not going to let another team take what is ours."[5]

Deschamps had some final advice for his players, too. He told them to get the ball to Mbappe.

Pogba did his part by scoring in the fifty-ninth minute. Then it was Mbappe's turn. Croatia was furiously trying to come back. Mbappe wanted to end its dreams.

CLINCHING THE CUP

As Lucas Hernandez worked the ball up the left sideline, he spotted Mbappe alone at the top of the 18-yard box. It was far out, but Mbappe had an accurate shot. Hernandez passed to Mbappe, who took one touch with the inside of his right foot. Then he used the outside of the same foot to put the ball in position. He stepped up to strike it. The keeper could not even get a hand on it. It went into the lower-left corner for a 4–1 lead. With 25 minutes to play, France all but had its fingers wrapped around the World Cup trophy.

Croatia added a goal, but it was too late. At the final whistle, the France players all ran onto the field and hugged in celebration. Mbappe could not stop smiling. He was presented with the Best Young Player award for

KIND SUPERSTAR

Just for winning the World Cup, Mbappe and his teammates each received a bonus of $350,000. Added to the bonuses for the other games they won, the total came to more than $500,000.[8] Mbappe chose to donate his winnings to charity. The charity of his choice was Premiers de Cordee, which organizes sporting events for children with disabilities. Mbappe also donates his time to the organization, making appearances and playing with the kids.

his performance at the World Cup. His four goals tied him for second most at the tournament.

It had been 60 years since someone as young as Mbappe scored in a World Cup final. That person was Pelé. The Brazilian great tweeted a message to Mbappe after the match. "If Kylian keeps equaling my records like this I may have to dust my boots off again," the 77-year-old legend said.[6]

"The king will always remain king," Mbappe replied.[7]

He was not only part of the future. He was a major part of France's present.

France's players toss Didier Deschamps in the air as they celebrate their World Cup victory.

RANE
4
DEMBELE
11
AREOLA
23
LEMAR
8
SIDIBE
19

MBAPPE
10

NATIONAL HERO

In 2018, a new image towered above the Bondy streets where Kylian Mbappe used to play as a boy. It was a picture of Mbappe in his PSG jersey. Behind his head were the words *Bondy Villes des Possibles*.

"Bondy, city of possibilities."

Mbappe went from small-town kid to World Cup hero. His life had changed in profound ways. He was suddenly one of the most famous people in France.

"My life has been totally turned upside down," he said. "I did not have the moments of so-called normal people during adolescence, like going out with friends, enjoying good times."[1]

But despite all that, Mbappe was living the life he had always dreamed of. He was playing the sport he loved at its highest level. And he was doing it for his country and for his hometown club.

CHAPTER NINE

Kylian Mbappe has become a hero to a new generation of French soccer fans.

NEW YEAR, NEW NUMBER

When PSG unveiled new white uniforms for the 2018–19 season, there was a surprise in the photos. Mbappe was sporting a new No. 7 on the back of his jersey. Mbappe had previously worn No. 29 with PSG. When Lucas Moura was sold to Tottenham Hotspur, Mbappe chose to take over No. 7. It's a legendary number in soccer, with many great players having worn it. One was Mbappe's childhood idol, Cristiano Ronaldo.

"For a long time, I said that numbers were unimportant and that it was something that only matters on the [field]," Mbappe said. "However, it is an indication of your ambitions—the player you want to become."[2]

DEFENDING THE TITLE

Expectations for Mbappe with PSG were even higher after his World Cup triumph. PSG wanted to defend its Ligue 1 title and go further in the Champions League. Mbappe hit the ground running.

A little over a month after beating Croatia, Mbappe scored two goals in his first Ligue 1 match of the 2018–19 season. PSG and Guingamp were tied 1–1 with ten minutes left when Mbappe scored the game winner. He went on to score in his next two matches as well.

PSG won all three, but the third one was marred by Mbappe receiving a red card. The card was for a dangerous tackle Mbappe made in stoppage time. He apologized for losing his temper but said he was defending himself. He said he was the victim of rough

Mbappe meets with the media to discuss the red card he was given during a game against Nimes on September 1, 2018.

treatment by opposing players from Nimes that the referee did not see.

Mbappe missed a match but was back for PSG's Champions League opener versus Liverpool. PSG trailed 2–1 late in the match when the ball fell to him and he buried it. With five goals in his first four matches, Mbappe

ULTIMATE PLAYER

Mbappe enjoys playing video games, especially the *FIFA* series of soccer games. As one of the best players in the world, he of course appears in the game himself. In the 2017 edition of the game, Mbappe was rated a 71 overall, out of 100. But with his breakthrough year, he got a 12-point boost in 2018. When the 2019 game came out, he was at 97. For speed, he was rated almost perfect at 99. That made him one of the best players to use in the game.[3]

was off to the best start of his career.

After another goal in the Champions League against Red Star Belgrade, Mbappe had maybe the best game of his career to that point. It was a league match against Olympique Lyonnais. He did something that hadn't been done in 45 years.

It was a strange game from the start. Both PSG and Lyon had a player ejected in the first half. Neymar had scored on a penalty to give PSG a 1–0 lead. As the match entered its final half hour, Mbappe took over.

In the sixty-first minute, he took a shot that bounced off the right post, bounced off the left post, and finally went in. Five minutes later, he was all alone in the box for a tap-in. Three minutes after that, it was as simple as could be. Mbappe used his blazing speed to run away from the defense and beat the keeper one-on-one.

That was the hat trick, but he still was not done. Five minutes later, the ball fell to him after several blocked PSG shots. He got the ball in for his fourth goal. That was four goals in 13 minutes of game action. He was the youngest player to score four goals in a Ligue 1 match in 45 years.

BECOMING THE BEST

By January, Mbappe had scored 16 goals. He was on pace to shatter his previous career high. PSG was undefeated in Ligue 1 and running away with the title. And they were in the Round of 16 in the Champions League. Life was good for Mbappe.

In December, Mbappe was named the best U-21 player in the world. He also came in fourth for the Ballon D'Or, presented to the overall best player in the world. It was

SOCIAL STAR

Mbappe loves to interact with fans on social media, especially the photo-sharing app Instagram. Mbappe had more than 25 million followers by January 2019. He gained approximately ten million of those followers since the World Cup.[5] Most often he likes to share pictures of himself hanging out with his friends and family. But he also posts images of his playing career, as well as some of the charity work he's doing. Mbappe had some fun with Cristiano Ronaldo in 2018. Mbappe once posted a picture on social media of his childhood bedroom, which was covered with Ronaldo posters. But Mbappe altered the photo in 2018 so that all the posters were of himself celebrating a fantastic year. The post earned nearly four million likes.[6]

MBAPPÉ
7
ooredoo

an incredible honor at such a young age. He had plenty of chances ahead to win one for himself.

From Bondy to Monaco to Paris to the World Cup final, Mbappe had been on quite a journey in his first 20 years. He delighted fans and frustrated opponents. And there was so much more of it to come.

FIRST PENALTY

Mbappe rarely takes penalty kicks for France. But he got his first international goal from the penalty spot in October 2018. It was a friendly against Iceland. Mbappe was not supposed to play. He was nursing an injury. But he came on for a half hour at the end with France losing 2–0. He first forced an Iceland own goal by firing a shot in off a defender. Then, after Iceland committed a handball, Mbappe stepped up and nailed the penalty. The match ended in a 2–2 draw.

Mbappe has had a successful young career.

TIMELINE

1998
Mbappe is born in Paris on December 20.

2004
Mbappe begins playing youth soccer in Bondy, his hometown near Paris.

2011
Mbappe begins playing at the prestigious Clairefontaine Academy.

2013
Mbappe joins the youth academy of AS Monaco.

2015
On December 2, Mbappe makes his senior team debut with Monaco, coming on as a substitute.

2016

February
Mbappe scores his first Ligue 1 goal on February 20, becoming the youngest-ever Monaco player to do so.

July
France wins the Under-19 European Championship.

December
Mbappe scores his first career hat trick in a 7–0 win over Rennes.

2017

Mbappe makes his first UEFA Champions League start and scores his first goal.

March

Mbappe makes his France team debut, coming on as a substitute against Luxembourg.

August

Mbappe scores his first international goal for France against the Netherlands; Paris Saint-Germain announces that Mbappe is joining the club.

October

Mbappe wins the Golden Boy award as the best player in Europe under 21.

2018

Mbappe scores two goals in the knockout round of the World Cup against Argentina and is named Man of the Match as France advances to the quarterfinals; Mbappe scores a goal in the World Cup final as France beats Croatia 4–2 and he is named Best Young Player of the tournament; Mbappe scores a career-high four goals in a span of just 13 minutes.

ESSENTIAL FACTS

FULL NAME
Kylian Adesanmi Mbappe Lottin

DATE OF BIRTH
December 20, 1998

PLACE OF BIRTH
Paris, France

PARENTS
Wilfried Mbappe and Fayza Lamari

EDUCATION
Clairefontaine Academy

CAREER HIGHLIGHTS

- Won the 2017 Under-19 European Championship and 2018 World Cup with France

- Named Best Young Player at the 2018 World Cup

- Won Ligue 1 in 2017 with AS Monaco and in 2018 with PSG

CONFLICTS

Through 2018, Mbappe had been issued two red cards in his career—on January 30, 2018, and September 1, 2018—both while playing for PSG.

QUOTE

"He has the clear-headedness to make choices, especially his calmness in one-on-ones with the goalkeeper. At a young age like that, that's very rare and it's why he is so clinical."

—France coach Didier Deschamps

GLOSSARY

aggregate
The whole sum or amount.

cap
An appearance in an international soccer game.

colony
A country that is the property of another country.

counterattack
When the defending team gets the ball and begins to attack on offense.

crossing pass
A pass delivered from the side of the field toward the middle.

draw
A game that ends in a tie.

dribbling
The touches on the ball by a player as it is taken up the field.

friendly
A match that is not part of league play or a tournament; an exhibition match.

group stage
The part of a tournament when teams are divided into smaller groups or pools; each team faces the others in the group, and those with the best records move on to the knockout stage.

hat trick
Three goals scored by the same player in one game.

heritage
Coming from a particular place or background.

knockout

The stage of a competition in which one loss eliminates a team.

own goal

A goal that is accidentally scored by a player against his or her own team.

relegated

Demoted from a higher league based on the results of the season.

rout

An instance where one team or individual defeats another badly.

stepover

A soccer move in which a player pretends to step over the ball but then kicks it in another direction.

stoppage time

Also known as added time, a number of minutes tacked on to the end of a half for stoppages that occurred during play from injuries, free kicks, and goals.

striker

A player whose primary responsibility is to create scoring chances and score goals.

tackle

A defensive move involving knocking a player down in order to take the ball away from that player.

trial

When a player is offered the chance to try out for a place on a club.

ADDITIONAL RESOURCES

SELECTED BIBLIOGRAPHY

Kuper, Simon. "Kylian Mbappe and the Curse of Winning a World Cup." *ESPN*, 28 Sept. 2018. espn.com. Accessed 11 Jan. 2019.

Smith, Rory, and Elian Peltier. "Kylian Mbappé and the Boys from the Banlieues." *New York Times*, 7 June 2018. nytimes.com. Accessed 11 Jan. 2019.

Walt, Vivienne. "Kylian Mbappe Is the Future of Soccer." *Time*, 10 Oct. 2018. time.com. Accessed 11 Jan. 2019.

FURTHER READINGS

Caioli, Luca, and Cyril Collot. *Mbappé*. London: Icon, 2018.

Caioli, Luca, and Cyril Collot. *Pogba, Mbappé, Griezmann: The French Revolution*. London: Icon, 2019.

Moussavi, Sam. *World Cup Heroes*. Minneapolis, MN: Abdo, 2019.

ONLINE RESOURCES

To learn more about Kylian Mbappe, please visit **abdobooklinks.com** or scan this QR code. These links are routinely monitored and updated to provide the most current information available.

MORE INFORMATION

For more information on this subject, contact or visit the following organizations:

LIGUE 1

6, rue Léo Delibes
75116 Paris, France
+33 1 53 65 38 00
ligue1.com

Ligue 1 has news articles about professional soccer teams so people can stay up-to-date on their favorite clubs.

NATIONAL FOOTBALL MUSEUM

Urbis Building
Cathedral Gardens, Todd St.
Manchester M4 3BG, United Kingdom
+44 0161 605 8200
nationalfootballmuseum.com

The National Football Museum has exhibitions, collections, and information on the history of soccer.

PARIS SAINT-GERMAIN FOOTBALL CLUB

Parc des Princes
24, rue Commandant Guilbaud
Paris, France
+33 01 47 43 71 71
en.psg.fr

Located at the Parc des Princes, the headquarters of PSG also includes a team store.

SOURCE NOTES

CHAPTER 1. COMEBACK KID

1. Christopher Clarey. "France and Argentina Meet in an Elite Battle for World Cup Survival." *New York Times*, 29 June 2018, nytimes.com. Accessed 11 Mar. 2019.

2. "World Cup: Kylian Mbappe—5 Things You Need to Know about the France Star Who Has the World at His Feet." *Straits Times*, 1 July 2018, straitstimes.com. Accessed 11 Mar. 2019.

3. Jonathan Wilson. "Kylian Mbappe Confirms World-Class Status in Leading France over Argentina." *Sports Illustrated*, 30 June 2018, si.com. Accessed 11 Mar. 2019.

CHAPTER 2. YOUTH CAREER

1. Emmanuelle Hingant. "UEFA.com's Weekly Wonderkid: Kylian Mbappé." *UEFA*, 13 Feb. 2016, uefa.com. Accessed 12 Mar. 2019.

2. John Bennett. "Kylian Mbappe: How France World Cup Star Rose to Prominence." *BBC*, 30 June 2018, bbc.com. Accessed 11 Mar. 2019.

3. Angelique Chrisafis. "France Pins Its Hopes on Kylian Mbappé, the Boy from the Banlieue." *Guardian*, 15 July 2018, theguardian.com. Accessed 12 Mar. 2019.

CHAPTER 3. MONACO ROOKIE

1. "Kylian Mbappe Offered Monaco Contract amid Arsenal, Liverpool Links." *ESPN*, 24 Feb. 2016, espn.com. Accessed 12 Mar. 2019.

2. "Kylian Mbappe Offered Monaco Contract amid Arsenal, Liverpool Links."

3. Dan Gibbs. "Confirmed: Man Utd, Arsenal and Liverpool Target Signs Contract Until 2019." *Express*, 8 Mar. 2016, express.co.uk. Accessed 12 Mar. 2019.

CHAPTER 4. WEARING THE BLUE

1. "Kylian Mbappé: The Fast Learner Who Takes It All in His Rapid Stride." *Guardian*, 13 July 2018, theguardian.com. Accessed 12 Mar. 2019.

2. Ashish Khanna. "Top 10: Most Watched Football Leagues in the World: Bundesliga Tops the List." *Inside Sport*, 26 June 2018, insidesport.co. Accessed 12 Mar. 2019.

CHAPTER 5. CHAMPION OF FRANCE

1. Jonathan Jurejko. "Kylian Mbappe Joins Paris St-Germain: Why an 18-Year-Old Is Worth €166m." *BBC*, 1 Sept. 2017, bbc.com. Accessed 12 Mar. 2019.

2. Robin Bairner. "'Son' Mbappe Is Priceless—Monaco Vice-President." *Goal*, 3 May 2017, goal.com. Accessed 12 Mar. 2019.

CHAPTER 6. LES BLEUS DEBUT

1. Ian Holyman. "Monaco Youngster Kylian Mbappe Gets First Senior France Call-Up." *ESPN*, 16 Mar. 2017, espn.com. Accessed 12 Mar. 2019.

2. Amy Lawrence. "Kylian Mbappé in Poll Position as France Urges Change after World Cup Loss." *Guardian*, 11 June 2017, theguardian.com. Accessed 12 Mar. 2019.

3. "Kylian Mbappe No Saviour of France ahead of World Cup Qualifier against Bulgaria." *National*, 5 Oct. 2017, thenational.ae. Accessed 12 Mar. 2019.

CHAPTER 7. BACK IN PARIS

1. Peter Hanson. "Monaco 1 Paris Saint-Germain 2: Dani Alves' Dream Debut Secures Trophee Des Champions." *Goal*, 29 July 2017, goal.com. Accessed 12 Mar. 2019.

2. Gill Clark. "Kylian Mbappe Says He Spoke to Real Madrid before PSG Transfer." *Bleacher Report*, 27 Dec. 2017, bleacherreport.com. Accessed 12 Mar. 2019.

3. Clark, "Kylian Mbappe Says He Spoke to Real Madrid before PSG Transfer."

4. Jonathan Johnson. "Monaco Star Kylian Mbappe, 18, Follows Neymar in Moving to PSG in Huge Deal." *ESPN*, 31 Aug. 2017, espn.com. Accessed 12 Mar. 2019.

5. Chris Burton. "Mbappe Hailed as PSG's Missing Link as Verratti Salutes Big-Money Signings." *Goal*, 28 Sept. 2017, goal.com. Accessed 12 Mar. 2019.

6. Burton, "Mbappe Hailed as PSG's Missing Link as Verratti Salutes Big-Money Signings."

7. Jonathan Johnson. "Kylian Mbappe Admits He Deserved Red Card in PSG's Defeat of Rennes." *ESPN*, 30 Jan. 2018, espn.com. Accessed 12 Mar. 2019.

8. Simon Kuper. "For Kylian Mbappe, the World's Best Player under 20, Life Moves Pretty Fast." *ESPN*, 12 Feb. 2018, espn.com. Accessed 12 Mar. 2019.

CHAPTER 8. BEST YOUNG PLAYER

1. Adeline Sire. "After France Won the 1998 World Cup, French Diversity Was Celebrated. But It Was Short-Lived." *PRI*, 29 June 2018, pri.org. Accessed 12 Mar. 2019.

2. Daniel Mumbere. "Weah, Drogba, Mbappe Launch Africa Sports Project in France." *Africa News*, 22 Feb. 2018, africanews.com. Accessed 12 Mar. 2019.

3. Simon Kuper. "Kylian Mbappe and the Curse of Winning a World Cup." *ESPN*, 28 Sept. 2018, espn.com. Accessed 12 Mar. 2019.

4. Chris Bevan. "Denmark–France." *BBC*, 26 June 2018, bbc.com. Accessed 12 Mar. 2019.

5. Alec Shilton. "Paul Pogba Gives Inspirational France Team Talk before Firing Them to Glory in World Cup Final." *Sun*, 19 July 2018, thesun.co.uk. Accessed 12 Mar. 2019.

6. @Pelé. "If Kylian keeps equaling my records like this I may have to dust my boots off again." *Twitter*, 15 July 2018, twitter.com. Accessed 12 Mar. 2019.

7. Yoni Blumberg. "Kylian Mbappe Will Donate $500,000 in Winnings to Charity—Here's How He Went from a Rough Neighborhood to the World Cup." *CNBC*, 16 July 2018, cnbc.com. Accessed 12 Mar. 2019.

8. Blumberg, "Kylian Mbappe Will Donate $500,000 in Winnings to Charity."

CHAPTER 9. NATIONAL HERO

1. "Kylian Mbappe: France Striker Features on Time Magazine Front Cover." *BBC*, 12 Oct. 2018, bbc.com. Accessed 12 Mar. 2019.

2. Jonathan Johnson. "Kylian Mbappe Gets No. 7 Shirt in New-Look Paris Saint-Germain Kit." *ESPN*, 26 July 2018, espn.com. Accessed 18 Mar. 2019.

3. Josh Lawless. "Kylian Mbappe's FIFA 19 Teams of the Year Card Is Pure Filth." *Sport Bible*, 7 Jan. 2019, sportbible.com. Accessed 12 Mar. 2019.

4. Simon Kuper. "Kylian Mbappe and the Curse of Winning a World Cup." *ESPN*, 28 Sept. 2018, espn.com. Accessed 12 Mar. 2019.

5. "K.mbappe." *Trackalytics*, n.d., trackalytics.com. Accessed 12 Mar. 2019.

6. "K.mbappe." *Instagram*, n.d., instagram.com. Accessed 12 Mar. 2019.

INDEX

ABOUT THE AUTHOR

Todd Kortemeier is a sportswriter, editor, children's book author, and soccer fan from Minnesota. A die-hard Tottenham Hotspur supporter, he lives near Minneapolis with his wife and dog.